Plant Adaptations

How We Live in Our Habitat

Written by Sarah Lalonde

This book is dedicated to Amanda and Steven. I am so happy to have you back in the States! Amanda, I am so proud of you completing your Master's in Environmental Sciences while in Okinawa. Steven, thank you for your service to our country as a Marine and for loving our daughter!

ISBN 978-1-7327072-3-8

Contents

Plant Needs	4
Habitats	5
Adaptations for the Arctic	6
Adaptations for the Desert	10
Adaptations for the Ocean	14
Adaptations for the Temperate Forest	18
Adaptations for the Wetlands	22
Adaptations for the Rainforest	26
Other Interesting Adaptations	29
Glossary	32
Index	33

What do all plants need to live?

All plants have five basic needs:

air 

sunlight 

water 

other nutrients (food) 

and the ability to reproduce.   

Plants live in many places on the Earth.
Plants have special parts that help them live in their habitat. They also have special things they can do that help them live. These are called adaptations.

What are habitats?

The earth has many kinds of habitats. A habitat is a place where an animal or plant grows naturally. Each habitat gives the plants or animals in it what they need to live.

Plants and animals that live together in a habitat make up a community. They help each other get what they need.

The Arctic

Arctic habitats are places that are very cold. Summers are short and sunny. Winters are long, dark, and cold. Arctic habitats get about four inches of water from rain or snow a year. There is a lot of wind. There are not many plants.

What adaptations do plants in the arctic need to live?

purple saxifrage

Plants grow close to the ground. They are often found behind rocks. It is warmer and safer from the wind there.

In the arctic, plants have roots that don't go far into the ground. This is because the ground is frozen.

Many plants in the arctic are red. Dark colors help the plant to absorb (get), more heat from the sun.

Bear berry plants have green leaves. These leaves turn red when it gets colder out. This plant has thick leaves that keep the heat and water in it for longer.

Bear berry plant

pasque flowers

Plants with flowers grow and bloom quickly. This helps them to reproduce during the short summer.

Like other arctic plants, pasque flowers grow close to the ground. They are covered with little, silky hairs that keep them warm.

Deserts

Deserts are places that get only a little bit of rain every year. They are usually hot, dry, and sandy.

What adaptations do plants in the desert need to live?

Many flowers in the desert rest when it is dry. After it rains these flowers bloom quickly. They are bright colors, so insects come to pollinate them. Flowers in the desert make seeds rapidly. Desert flowers have little hairs on their leaves that help keep the water in for longer.

Cactus in the Desert

saguaro cactus

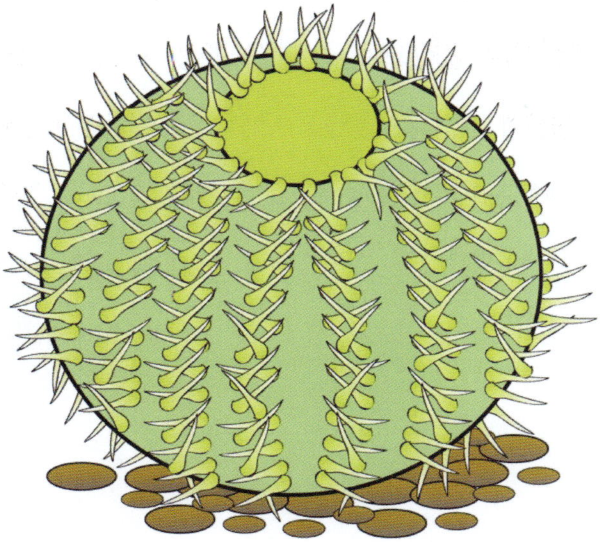

barrel cactus

aloe

There are many kinds of cacti in the desert.

Some cacti have roots that grow deep in the ground. These cacti get water deep in the ground. Other cacti have roots near the top of the ground. They can get water quickly when it rains. Cacti grow far apart so that they can get water and nutrients from a large area.

Cacti have thick stems. The stems keep water in them for a long time.

Most cacti do not have leaves. They have spikes (thorns). They do not lose as much water as plants with leaves do. Spikes also keep animals from eating them.

The seeds of a cactus grow very quickly to help it reproduce.

Oceans

Ocean water covers more of the Earth than land does. Ocean water moves all the time. Water in the ocean is salty.

What adaptations do plants in the ocean need to live?

Only a few plants can live in the ocean. Most of them are small living things called plankton. These make half of the oxygen for the animals on the Earth. Plankton are too little to be seen. People see groups of plankton when they clump together. They have flat bodies and spines. This helps them to float.

plankton

seaweed

There are many kinds of seaweed in the ocean. Some seaweed has special roots that keep them hooked to rocks. This way they can stay in one place when the water moves. Most seaweed has thick, flexible skin that protects them from waves. This thick skin also keeps them from drying out in the sun. Some seaweed has air sacks to help them float. Other seaweed plants stick together to make floating mats. Floating on the water lets them get energy from the sun so they can make their own food. Being in a floating mat also helps this plant to reproduce.

Seagrass lives in the water near the shore. Seagrass is the only flowering plant that can live underwater. The seagrass flowers make seeds that are moved by ocean waves. They have stems under the ocean floor. Roots grow down from these stems keeping these plants in place. Seagrass leaves are flexible. They bend as the water moves around them. Seagrass reaches up to get light from the sun.

All sea plants must adapt to salt water.

seagrass

Temperate Forests

Temperate forests don't get too hot or too cold. There are four seasons in areas with forests. They get lots of rain. The soil there is good because there are many rotting leaves. Many things can live in the forest.

What adaptations do plants in the temperate forests need to live?

Thick bark on trees helps protect them against cold weather. Trees have roots that spread out under the ground. The roots can get lots of water and other nutrients from the soil.

The leaves of most trees are thin and wide. This helps them to get sunlight in warm weather. They use the sunlight to make food. The trees save some of the food for cold weather. The leaves fall off in the winter. This helps the plant lose less water. The trees have adapted to grow new leaves in the spring.

maple tree seed

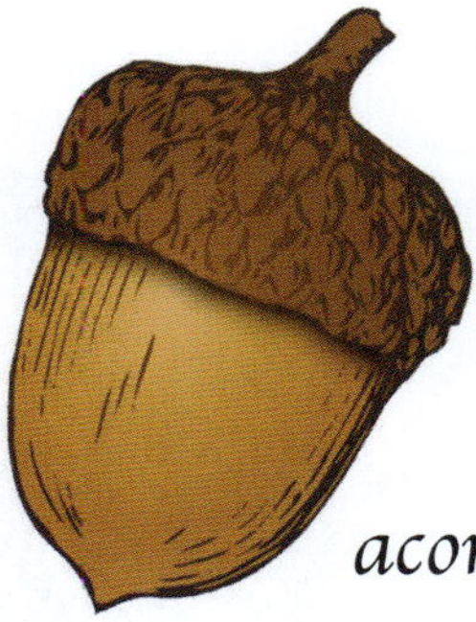

acorn

In the forest seeds need to move away from their parents. The seeds have a better chance of getting the sunlight that they need to grow. Maple tree seeds move when it is windy. Squirrels and other animals take acorns away from oak trees and bury them. Pine trees have cones with seeds. These seeds are eaten by animals. They come out in their scat (poop). The seeds have adapted to start to grow when it is very warm.

pine cones

ferns

Ferns have small leaves called leaflets. Leaflets help them to live when the temperature changes. The small leaflets fall off when winter comes. Fern stems are under the ground. The stems put out little roots. New plants grow from the roots.

Flowers grow on the forest floor before tree leaves come out. This way they get the sun they need.

moss

wildflowers

Moss lives by storing water and nutrients. They have adapted to live close to the ground.

Wetlands

Wetland habitats are areas that are covered with shallow water. The soil is very wet. People sometimes call these areas swamps or marshes. Many plants and animals live in and near wetlands.

What adaptations do plants in the wetlands need to live?

Water lilies have many of the adaptations that plants living in the wetlands need. The leaves and stems under water can bend. They move when the water moves. They have space for air in their stems that help them stay up. The flat, wide leaves on top of the water help them float. The leaves get light from the sun. Many water lilies have thorns on the bottoms of their leaves. The thorns protect them from predators, such as fish.

Cattails live in wetlands. The thin, long leaves can sway with the water. Cattails have a long, brown flower. These flowers make very small seeds with tiny hairs. The wind helps to move the seeds. The seeds can float on the water. Cattails have stems under the ground that send out little roots. New plants grow from these roots, too.

swamp thistle

Swamp thistles are adapted for life in the wetlands. Their flowers, stems, and leaves are prickly. This stops animals from eating them. They have long thick roots that go deep into the ground. This makes it easier for them to live when the water moves. Swamp thistle seeds are moved by wind.

Rainforests

Rainforests are warm habitats. Rainforests get more rain than any other place. Rainforests get more than a hundred inches of rain in a year. Half of the plants and animals in the world live in rainforests.

What adaptations do plants in the rainforest need to live?

Often, trees in the rainforest have buttress roots. These are large, wide roots all around the trees. Trees have smooth thin bark. This helps water to leave the tree quickly.

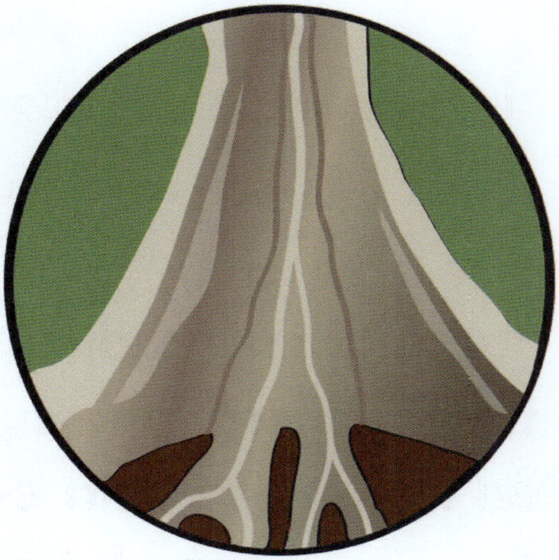

buttress roots

leaf with a drip tip

Many leaves in the rainforest are wide and have a drip tip. This tip lets the water run off quickly. Plants in the rainforest need to get rid of water they don't need so that they don't get sick.

vines

Some vines have roots in the ground and climb up the tree towards the sun. Other vines grow at the top of the trees in the rainforest and drop their roots down into the soil.

Air plants, some kinds of flowers, and some ferns grow on other plants. They still get nutrients, sunlight, water, and air on their own. Growing on other plants helps them to stay in one place.

plants growing on another plant

Other Interesting Adaptations

Did you know that some plants have behavioral adaptations just like animals do?

Camouflage is a behavior. When something blends in with what is around it, it is camouflaged. Living stone plants have a shape and color that help them blend in with what is around them.

living stone plant

Mimicry is a behavior. Mimicry is when one living thing acts or looks like another living thing. This behavior helps it to meet its needs.

Bee Orchids look like a female bee. This gets the male bees to come pollinate them.

Skunk cabbage smells like a skunk. The smell brings insects that like to eat rotting meat. The bugs pollinate the cabbage.

Sundews are meat eating plants. The drops on them look like dew drops. The drops are not dew. Insects land on the flowers to drink "the dew." The insects get trapped and eaten.

Migration is an adaptation. When living things migrate, they move to places that are better for them. When seeds travel, they migrate.

coconut floating on the water

Glossary

adaptation - a body part, covering, or behavior that helps a plant or an animal live in its habitat

behavior - the way a living thing acts

camouflage - color or shape of a living thing that helps it blend into its habitat

habitat – a natural space for something to live in

migration - the act of moving from one place to another

needs – things you must have to live

nutrient - food

reproduce - to make new organisms

Index

A

adaptation, 4, 7, 11, 15, 19, 23, 27, 29
air, 4, 16, 23, 28
arctic, 6,7,8,9

D

desert, 10, 11, 12, 13

F

flower, 9, ,11, 16, 21, 24, 25, 28, 31

H

habitat, 4, 5, 6, 22, 26

L

leaves, 8, 13, 17, 18, 19, 21, 23, 24, 25, 27

N

nutrient, 4, 13, 19, 21, 28

O
ocean, 14, 15, 16

R
rainforest, 26, 27, 28
reproduce, 4, 9, 13, 16
roots, 2, 13, 16, 17, 19, 21, 24, 25, 27, 28

S
seeds, 11, 13, 17, 20, ,24, 31
stems, 13, 17, 21, 23, 24, 25
sunlight, 4, 19 20, 28

T
temperate forest, 12, 19

W
water, 4, ,8, 13, 14, 16, 17, 19, 21, 22, 23, 24, 27, 28
wetlands, 22, 23, 24, 25

Printed in Great Britain
by Amazon

33309107R00021